101 QUESTIONS & ANSWERS

WHO? WHAT? WHERE? WHY?

Our Planet Earth

HAMLYN

GLOSSARY

atmosphere The layer of air around the Earth. It gets thinner with height, and fades away at about 100-200 km into the nothingness of space.

axis The imaginary line around which the Earth spins, once each day. It goes through the centre of the Earth and the North and South poles.

core The central part or middle of the Earth, about 5,000 km across, and made of melted rocks and metals.

crust The outermost layer of the Earth, made of solid rock, and covered by mountains and seas.

current In the ocean, the large-scale movement or flow of water, caused by the Earth's spinning motion, wind, and the warming effects of the Sun.

Equator An imaginary line around the middle of the Earth, at its widest point, halfway between the North and South Poles. The weather is warm there all year round.

fold A huge curve or bend in the rocks of the Earth's crust. High folds are known as mountains.

fossil The remains of a long-dead animal, plant or other once-living thing, which have been buried in the rocks and turned to stone.

geology The general study of rocks, the Earth's crust and the changing landscape.

igneous A type of rock made when the original rock gets so hot that it melts, then cools and goes hard and solid again.

lava Red-hot, melted, runny rock that oozes or spurts from a volcano.

magma Red-hot, melted, runny rock that is under the Earth's surface.

magnetic North Pole The place at which a compass needle points. It is near, but not at, the true North Pole. It changes its position over the years.

mantle The middle layer of the Earth, between the crust on the outside and the core in the centre. It is almost 3,000 km thick.

metamorphic A type of rock made by changing the mineral and crystal structure of the original rock, due to pressure and heat, but without the original rock melting.

molten Melted into a runny liquid, as with magma in a volcano.

North Pole The "Top of the World", the upper point around which the Earth spins on its axis. It is opposite the South Pole, and its region is known as the Arctic. *See also* magnetic North Pole.

sedimentary A type of rock made when small particles settle in layers in water, or in a desert, get squashed by more layers settling above, and are cemented into solid rock.

South Pole The "Bottom of the World", the lower point around which the Earth spins on its axis. It is opposite the North Pole, and its region is known as the Antarctic.

stalactite An icicle-shaped object of minerals that hangs from the roof of a cave, and grows very slowly.

stalagmite A tall, pointed object of minerals that sticks up from the floor of a cave, and grows very slowly.

tectonic plate One of the gigantic, curved blocks of rock that make up the surface of the Earth, and that drift along slowly.

volcano A "leak" in the Earth's surface, where gases and incredibly hot melted rock spurt from deep below, through a hole called a vent.

First published in Great Britain in 1993 by
Hamlyn Children's Books
an imprint of Reed Children's Books
Michelin House, 81 Fulham Road
London SW3 6RB and Auckland, Melbourne, Singapore and Toronto.

This paperback edition published in 1994

Copyright © Reed International Books 1993

Designed and Produced by Lionheart Books, London

ISBN 0-600-58385-6

British Library Cataloguing-in-Publication Data. A catalogue record for this book is available from the British Library.

Printed in Italy

Acknowledgements
Designer: Ben White
Project Editor: Lionel Bender
Text-Editor: Madeleine Samuel
Media Conversion and Typesetting: Peter MacDonald and Una Macnamara
Managing Editor: David Riley
Production Controller: Ruth Charlton

Artwork: pages 4-5, 7b, 8-9b, 10l, 13c, 18t, 19, 21, 25, 26, 27, by Hayward Art Group; 5tr, 6, 7t, 11b, 13t, 15, 16, 17, 20, 22, 23, 24, 28-29, 39l, 46bl by Peter Bull Art Studio; 8-9t by Nick Shewing; 9t, 33b by Roger Courthold; 10r, 13b, 34, 35 by Brian Watson; 11t, 12, 14b, 18b, 23t, 28, 29r, 30-31, 32, 33t, 40, 42t, 43b, 44, 46t, 47t by Jason Lewis; 14t by Brian McIntyre; 31 by Maltings Partnership; 36, 38l, 39b by Ann Winterbotham; 36-37, 38r by John Rignall; 40-41, 42, 43t, 44-45 by John Martin Artists/Steve Holden; 46-47 by Bernard Thornton Artists/Fred Anderson. (top = top, b = bottom, l = left, r = right, c = centre).

CONTENTS

This book contains questions and answers on the following topics:

Steve Parker

Was Earth always the same and is it stable now?

No. In fact, the Earth has not always been here. It formed billions of years ago, from clouds of dust whirling in space. And as soon as it formed, it began to alter. If you could fly high in a plane, on the edge of space, you would be able to see the main features of the Earth's surface — and how they were made. Volcanoes erupt and build mountains. The rock layers at the surface squash together, tilt, buckle, and twist. Waves eat away at the coastline. New rocks form under the oceans. The Earth is so massive to us, that it seems still and never-changing. But it is really moving and ever-changing, sometimes on a grand scale, as this book will show.

DID YOU KNOW...
● That the Earth is not exactly round? It is slightly flattened top-to-bottom at the poles, and slightly bulging at the Equator around the middle.
● The Earth measures 12,714 km from the North Pole down through the middle to the South Pole?
● It is more from one side of the Equator, through the centre, to the other, at 12,756 km?
● It would take 14 months non-stop to walk right around the middle of the Earth, at the Equator — even if you could get across the water? This distance is 40,075 km.
● The distance right around the Earth from the North Pole to the South Pole and back again, is slightly less, at 40,008 km?

WHAT IS A VOLCANO?
The Earth leaks at holes like pimples across its surface. We call them volcanoes! New rocks form as liquid rocks well up under the sea bed, harden, move sideways, and squash the land. Holes and cracks form in the land, and red-hot, runny rock gushes out from deep inside.

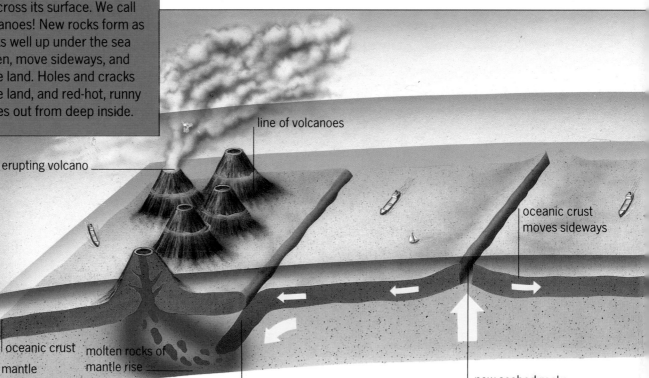

line of volcanoes

erupting volcano

oceanic crust moves sideways

oceanic crust

mantle

molten rocks of mantle rise

oceanic crust moves down into mantle and melts

new seabed rocks form oceanic crust

WHAT'S DEEP IN THE EARTH?

The Earth has five main layers. The outside one is the crust. Its thickness varies from about 6 to 60 km. Cut open an apple, and see how thin the skin is. Compared to its size, the Earth's crust is even thinner than the apple's skin.

What's under the crust?

The next two layers are the upper mantle and the lower mantle. The rocks are so hot that they bend like plastic and flow like treacle. Together the two mantle layers are almost 3,000 km thick.

What's at the centre?

Below the lower mantle is the outer core, about 2,200 km thick. In the very middle is the inner core, 2,500 km across. The centre of the Earth is solid, made mainly of the metals iron and nickel. With a temperature of 4,500°C, it is far too hot to imagine!

The upper mantle is solid, the lower mantle molten and plastic-like. The outer crust is liquid, the inner crust solid.

upper mantle
lower mantle
outer core
inner core
crust

continental crust

oceanic crust

The crust is thicker under the continents (land masses), than it is under the sea bed.

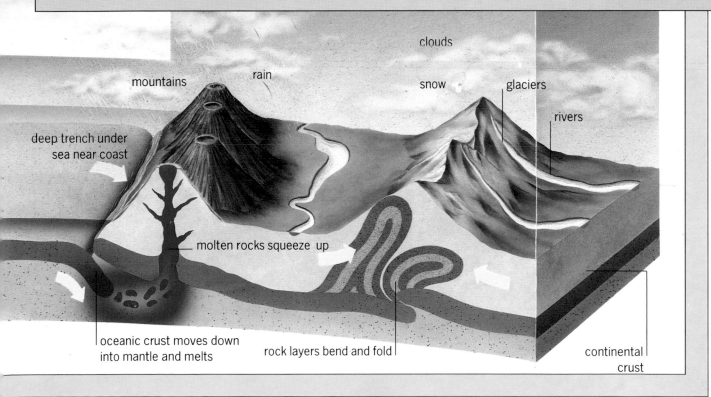

clouds

mountains
rain
snow
glaciers
rivers

deep trench under sea near coast

molten rocks squeeze up

oceanic crust moves down into mantle and melts

rock layers bend and fold

continental crust

Does Earth have neighbours?

Yes, eight of them. But they are not very near neighbours! Like the Earth, they are planets and they go around the Sun, which is a star. The nearest to us is Venus, then Mars. The biggest planet is Jupiter, and the most distant is tiny Pluto.

The nearer the planet to the Sun, the faster it completes each circuit or orbit. Mercury takes 28 days, Mars 687 days, Saturn 29 years, and Pluto 248 years. The Earth takes 365 days, which is how we measure our year.

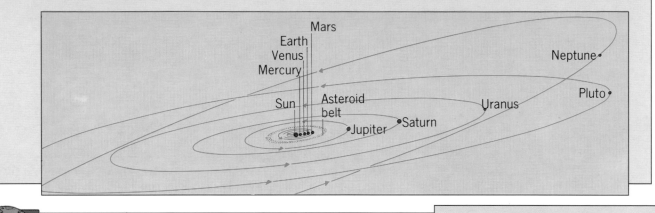

What makes seasons?

Seasons depend on the Earth orbiting the Sun, and the weather patterns this creates. In some places, the Sun's warmth makes winds blow from land to sea at one time of year. The air is cool and dry, so it is the dry season. As the Earth continues its orbit, the winds change and blow in from the sea, carrying moisture. This is the rainy season.

WHERE'S WETTEST?
● The rainiest place on Earth is Tutunendo, Colombia, South America. It has 11,770 mm of rain each year.
● The place with the most rainy days is Mount Wai-ale-ale, on the Hawaiian Islands, in the Pacific Ocean. It has only 15 dry days each year.

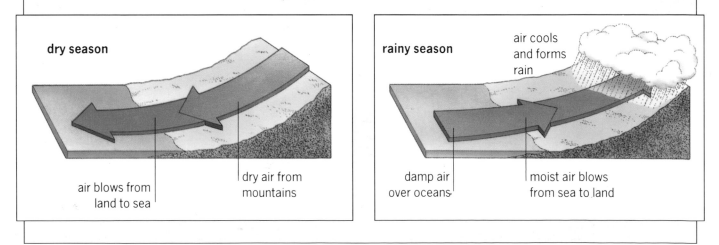

Why is it hot in summer?

The Earth orbits the Sun once each year. It also spins like a top, once each day. But the line around which the Earth spins, called its axis, is not upright compared to the Sun. It is tilted to one side. For about half the year, the northern parts of the Earth lean towards the Sun. They get the strongest sunlight and warmth, and so it is summer there. As the Earth continues its orbit, the southern parts become closer. This means it is summer there, and winter in the northern parts.

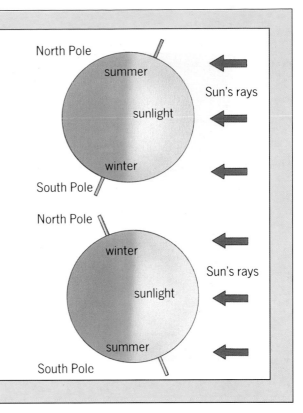

What is a rainbow?

It is a trick of the light. When light passes from one substance to another, such as from air to water, it is bent slightly. A rainbow forms when raindrops split sunlight into its different colours of the spectrum. Each colour is bent by a different amount, with violet being bent the most. The bending of light is known as refraction.

HOW LONG DOES IT LAST?
The longest-lasting rainbow was over three hours, in Wales in 1979. There may have been longer-lasting rainbows, but no one has recorded them scientifically. They fade away as the rainclouds blow along – and when the Sun goes in!

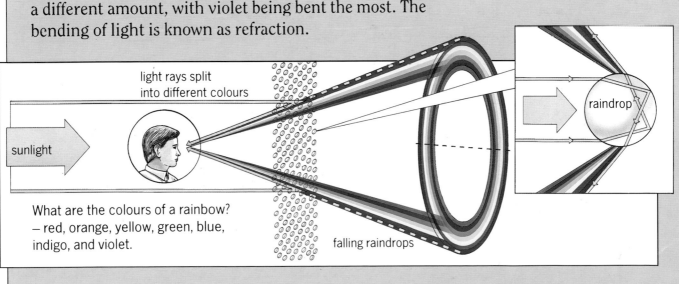

light rays split into different colours

sunlight

raindrop

What are the colours of a rainbow? – red, orange, yellow, green, blue, indigo, and violet.

falling raindrops

How do explorers find their way?

In strange lands or on the high seas, a compass is a vital instrument. It consists of a small magnetized needle that always swings around to point at the Earth's North and South Poles. This is because the Earth itself is like a giant magnet. Invisible lines of magnetic force pass through the air and ground. The Earth's North Pole attracts the south pole of the compass needle or other magnet.

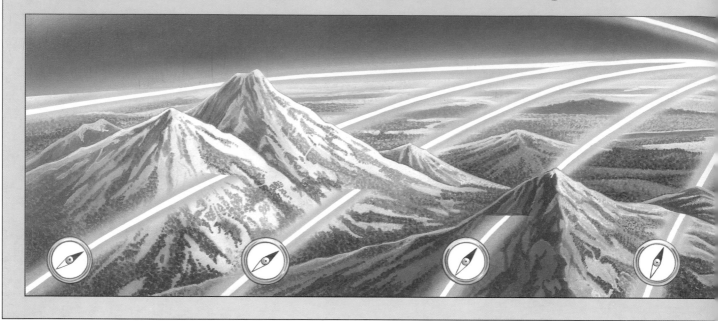

Can a compass be used in space?

The Earth's magnetic field extends far above the surface, out into space. It gets much weaker farther from the planet. It also gets disturbed by various rays and particles coming from the Sun, called the solar wind. And it gets disturbed by the van Allen belts, doughnut-shaped areas of electrified particles within the magnetic field. So if you relied on a compass, you would soon be lost in space!

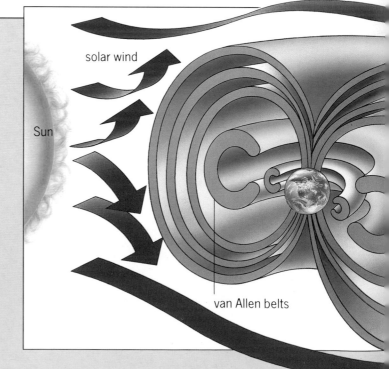

solar wind

Sun

van Allen belts

Animals such as birds and fish can detect the Earth's magnetism. They use it to find their way long distances, as they migrate from one region of land or sea to another.

CAN A COMPASS BE WRONG?

Through history, the North and South Poles have "wandered" around the top and bottom of the Earth, by hundreds of kilometres. This is because the magnetic field tilts and moves very slowly, due to gigantic currents of liquid rock flowing in the outer core region. So compasses must be regularly checked, and maps are updated with the new positions of the magnetic North and South Poles, as well as the true geographic North and South Poles, which stay still.

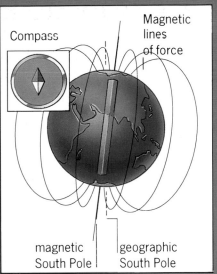

Compass

Magnetic lines of force

magnetic South Pole

geographic South Pole

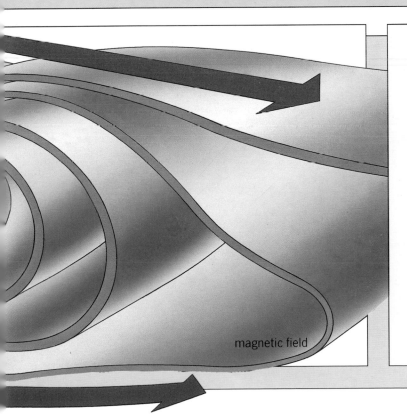

magnetic field

DID YOU KNOW...

● The solar wind blowing through the Earth's magnetosphere acts like a colossal generator, creating 100 billion watts of electrical power? If this could be gathered and used, it would help to solve our energy problems here on Earth!

● The van Allen belts are named after scientist James van Allen? They were first detected by the first US space satellites *Explorer 1* and *Explorer 3* in 1958. Van Allen led the team that worked on the information sent back from the satellites, including readings from radiation-detecting Geiger counters. The satellite *Explorer 12* brought back more information on the van Allen belts in 1961. Mercury, Jupiter and Saturn also have a magnetic field.

How high is space?

The air we breathe is thickest, or densest, at the Earth's surface. It gets thinner as you go higher, which is why high-altitude pilots and balloonists wear oxygen masks. The layer of air around the Earth is called the atmosphere. It has almost faded away into nothingness at the height of about 100 km. Above this is the near-vacuum of space, with a few particles floating around – and the odd satellite and rocket.

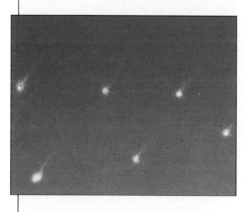

What is the ozone layer?
The layers of the atmosphere are shown on the right. The ozone layer protects the Earth's surface from damaging ultraviolet rays from the Sun.

Why do stars shoot?
Shooting stars are not real stars, though they "shoot" across the sky. They are usually rocky lumps that burn up as a fiery streak as they fall into the atmosphere.

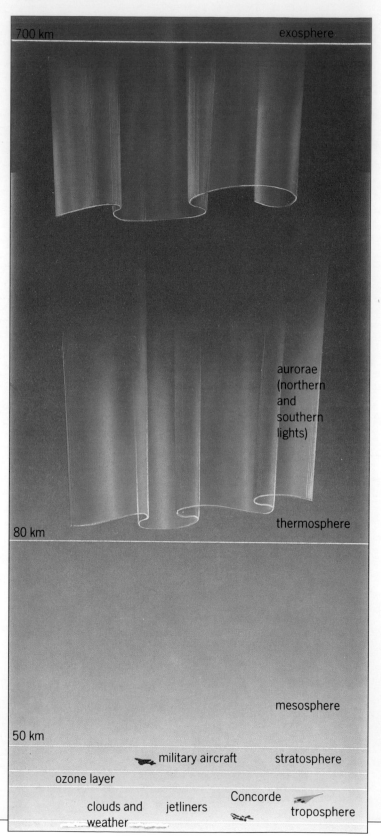

700 km — exosphere

aurorae (northern and southern lights)

thermosphere

80 km

mesosphere

50 km

military aircraft — stratosphere

ozone layer

clouds and weather — jetliners — Concorde — troposphere

What makes winds?

The Sun's warmth heats up different parts of the atmosphere, with the passing days and seasons. Warmed air rises, and cool air moves along to take its place. The Earth's spinning motion twists the main winds, as shown.

WINDS FROM OR TO?

Winds are named by the direction they blow from, not the direction they blow to. A northerly wind comes from the north, and blows towards the south. In Europe, a north wind brings very cold air from the polar regions. This is why people say: "The North wind doth blow, and we shall have snow."

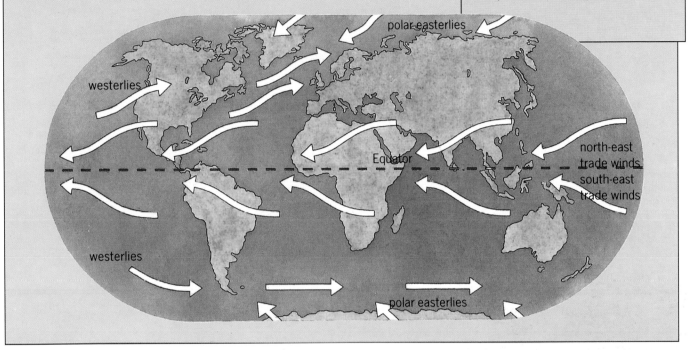

Why does weather vary?

Mid-way between the Equator and poles, the weather often changes from day to day. This is because warm air from the Equator meets cold air from the poles. The air masses move and swirl, bringing changeable weather.

WHERE'S WINDIEST?

Commonwealth Bay, on the southern continent of Antarctica, has gales with windspeeds of more than 300 km per hour. In a tornado, swirling winds of 450 km per hour cause immense damage as they lift cars, roofs and whole houses.

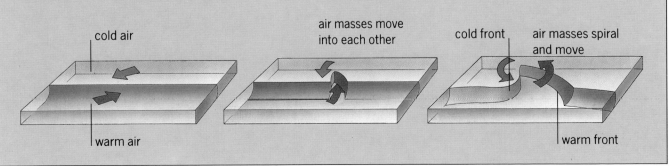

11

Why do winds prevail?

The Sun warms the air more at the Equator than at the Poles, setting up a pattern of air movements and winds. Added to this is the turning motion of the Earth, where the surface moves from west to east. These two factors create regular flows of air, which cause "prevailing" winds that blow regularly from a certain direction, for each place on the surface. Here, the patterns are shown for the northern hemisphere.

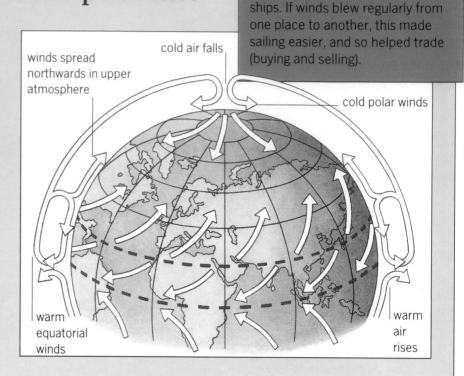

winds spread northwards in upper atmosphere

cold air falls

cold polar winds

warm equatorial winds

warm air rises

WHY "TRADE" WINDS?
In the olden days, goods were carried around the world by sailing ships. If winds blew regularly from one place to another, this made sailing easier, and so helped trade (buying and selling).

Could I drift across the ocean?

Yes, but only with a good safe craft, and only in a certain direction! In the same way that moving air is a wind, moving water is a current. The Sun's warmth and the Earth's spinning set up regular patterns of oceans currents, as they do for world winds. These currents, plus the winds blowing above the waves, carry floating objects for thousands of kilometres.

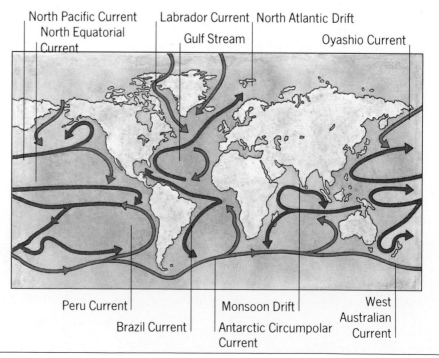

North Pacific Current
North Equatorial Current

Labrador Current
Gulf Stream

North Atlantic Drift
Oyashio Current

Peru Current

Brazil Current

Monsoon Drift

Antarctic Circumpolar Current

West Australian Current

Why does the sea go up and down?

Every lump of matter has a natural pulling force called gravity. The Moon's gravitational force pulls on the water in the oceans, making it bulge towards the Moon. As the Earth spins, the bulge of water travels around the Earth. This creates the rise and fall of the tides.

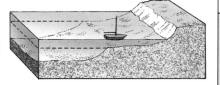

Moon's gravity pulls a bulge of water towards it, creating high tide. The movement causes another bulge on the opposite side.

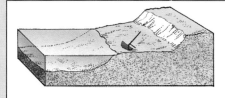

Low tide occurs between the bulges of water. This happens about twice each day.

tidal range 14.5 m in Bay of Fundy, Canada

As the Earth turns beneath the bulges, high tide happens in the middle of the bulge.

What is tidal power?

The movement of the tides is an immense amount of energy, which can be captured and turned into electricity for heat, light, cooking and industry. The world's first tidal power station is at the mouth of the River Rance, near St Malo in Brittany, France. As the water surges past with each tide, it flows though a dam or barrage, and turns huge turbine blades linked to electricity generators.

Why is the Earth like a jigsaw?

The Earth's surface layer or crust is not in one piece, like the shell of a coconut. It is made up of curved pieces called tectonic plates, that fit together into a ball-shaped jigsaw. There are about eight major plates, and several smaller ones, shown on the map below. They are named after the land masses or islands on them. And the plates are not still, but moving about very slowly, a few centimetres each year. This means the main land masses or continents are carried about on their plates, drifting to and fro across the planet. So the world map has changed in the past and will continue to change.

HOW DID THE PLATES FORM?
In the beginning, the Earth was a mass of flowing liquid rocks. Gradually the rocks in the crust cooled and took up their plate pattern, and began to drift.

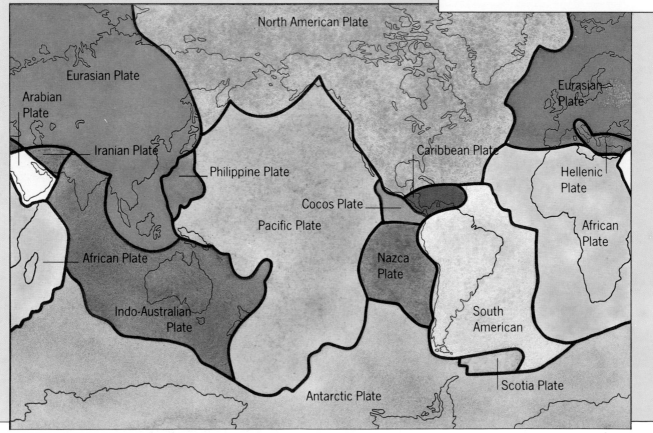

North American Plate

Eurasian Plate

Arabian Plate

Iranian Plate

Philippine Plate

African Plate

Indo-Australian Plate

Pacific Plate

Cocos Plate

Nazca Plate

Caribbean Plate

Eurasian Plate

Hellenic Plate

African Plate

South American

Scotia Plate

Antarctic Plate

Which pieces move most?

In general, there is most plate activity around the Pacific Ocean. As the plates move, they rub and squeeze against each other. This buckles and distorts them, and also opens up holes that we know as volcanoes, and causes immense shudders we call earthquakes. There are several chains of volcanoes and earthquakes zones around the Pacific.

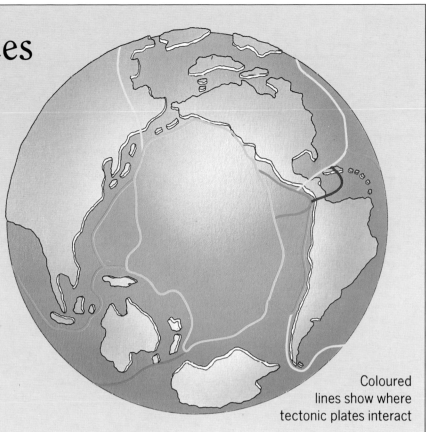

Coloured lines show where tectonic plates interact

Can new jigsaw pieces form?

Yes, molten rock from deep in the mantle wells up to the surface, mainly along cracks in the ocean floor. It hardens into solid rock and makes new plates of thin oceanic crust. These spread sideways, in the process known as seafloor spreading. Sometimes the continent-carrying plate is forced down under the oceanic one (1). Or the two plates may meet head on and jam together (2). If the continental plate is very heavy, it may force the oceanic plate underneath it (3). The oceanic plate slides back into the mantle and melts.

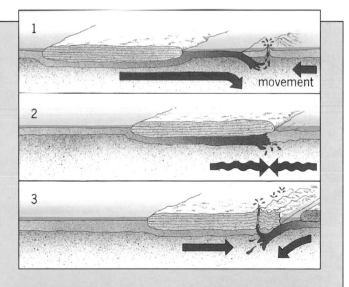

HOW MUCH WATER?

The Earth's total surface area is 510 million sq km. Of this, about 362 million sq km (almost 71 per cent) is covered by water. The biggest ocean is the Pacific, which covers 166 million sq km. It is almost as big as all the other oceans and seas added together.

Can land bend?

Yes, it can. Very few parts of the landscape are truly flat. Even if the surface looks flat, the rock layers beneath may be bent. Most places have hills and valleys, cliffs and canyons. These are caused by weather wearing away the rocks, and also by plate and crust movements bending them into folds over areas many kilometres wide.

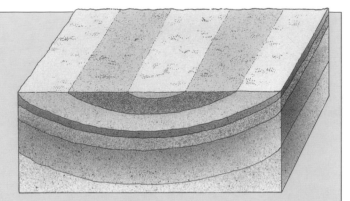
downward sag is a syncline

upward arch is an anticline

CAN YOU SEE THE BENDS?
The bends in the rocks, called folds, are best seen at places such as cliffs, beaches and quarries. Here the rock is cut away and laid bare. Sometimes the rocks are twisted and tilted right over, so that the type of rock on the surface in one place, is deep below the ground a few kilometres away.

Can the land crack?

Under the immense strain from crust and plate movements, the rock layers sometimes crack open. The cracks are known as faults or rifts. A block of rock may rise or fall between two faults, forming a hill or valley.

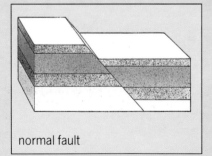
normal fault

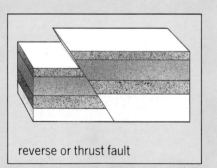
reverse or thrust fault

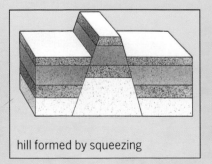
hill formed by squeezing

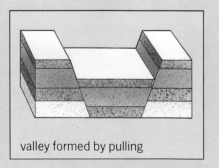
valley formed by pulling

HOW LONG?
The Great Rift Valley in East Africa is a spectacular series of cracks and faults, extending for more than 4,000 km.

How do mountains grow?

There are several types of mountains, made in different ways. Volcanic mountains, formed from new rock, are described on pages 18 and 19. Fold mountains are shown on the right. They are gigantic folds and wrinkles formed when the edge of a continent is distorted by movement of plates forming the Earth's crust. Block mountains described below are like huge, long wedges formed by faulting (opposite). Even as the mountains grow up, a few centimetres or metres each year, ice and wind and weather wear them down. This is the process of erosion.

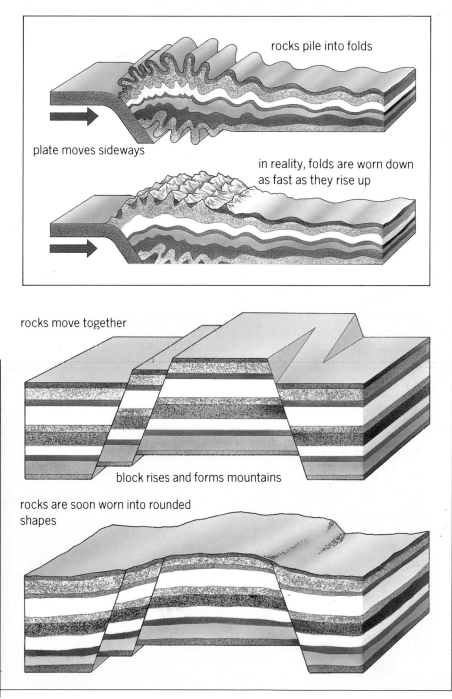

rocks pile into folds

plate moves sideways

in reality, folds are worn down as fast as they rise up

rocks move together

block rises and forms mountains

rocks are soon worn into rounded shapes

WHERE CAN I STAND ON TOP OF THE WORLD?
● The highest place on the Earth's surface is the summit of Mount Everest, in the Himalayas on the Tibet-Nepal border. It is 8,863 m above average sea level.
● The next highest is the top of Chogori or K2, a mountain in the Kashmiri area of north Pakistan. It is 8,607 m above sea level.
● Mauna Kea on Hawaii is 4,205 m above sea level but its sides go far below the sea. Its total height is 10,203 m.

What makes lava flow from volcanoes?

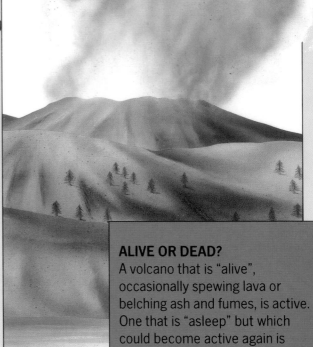

As the plates of the Earth's surface drift on the semi-liquid rock below, following gigantic "rock currents", they slide past and push against each other. This opens cracks and holes at weak points in the crust. Deep below is liquid rock called magma, in the mantle. The magma is under enormous pressure. It forces its way up any hole or crack it can find towards the surface, and bursts out as red-hot flowing rock, lava, from a volcano.

The map shows the world's main earthquake zones. Basaltic lava comes from tectonic plates being made, and andesitic lava from their destruction.

ALIVE OR DEAD?
A volcano that is "alive", occasionally spewing lava or belching ash and fumes, is active. One that is "asleep" but which could become active again is known as dormant. A volcano that is "dead", never erupting again, is called an extinct volcano.

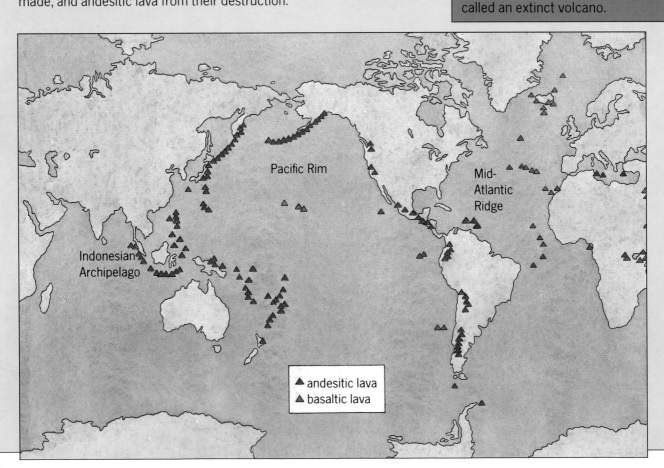

Pacific Rim

Mid-Atlantic Ridge

Indonesian Archipelago

▲ andesitic lava
▲ basaltic lava

WHICH IS THE BIGGEST VOLCANO?
● The tallest occasionally active volcano is Ojos del Salado, 6,890 m tall, on the border between Argentina and Chile, in South America.
● The biggest active volcano is probably Mauna Loa in Hawaii, in the Pacific Ocean. It is 4,168 m high, and the hardened lava has formed a dome 50 km wide and 120 km long.
● In modern times, the biggest ever volcanic eruption was on Krakatoa, a small island between Sumatra and Java, South-East Asia. It blew apart in 1883 and caused massive waves that killed more than 35,000 people.

LOST A MOUNTAIN?
The dormant volcano called Mount St Helens, in Washington State, north-west USA, woke up on 18 May 1980. A massive explosion blew away the side of the mountain, making it 400 m shorter, and filling the skies with clouds of ash and dust that altered the sunshine and sunsets halfway around the world. Despite warnings, several people died in the blast. The mountain had been dormant since 1857.

mountain before the eruption

side eruption

ash and fumes

vent

lava

cone

side vent

hardened layers of rock

magma chamber

WHAT'S INSIDE A VOLCANO?
A typical steep-sided, cone-shaped volcano has a central tube called a vent. The lava flows up from a magma chamber deep in the Earth. It may also seep out of side vents. With each eruption, the lava hardens and forms another layer, making the mountain higher. The lava hardens in many forms, like those shown below.

ropy lava

block lava

lava bombs

pillow lava

How can the Earth shake and vibrate?

When tectonic plates try to push or slide against each other, the rocks may be held together by their jagged shapes and the immense friction. But the plates suddenly "give" at a fault, slip and slide, and cause the shock waves, shaking and vibrations of an earthquake.

HOW STRONG?
The strength of an earthquake felt at different places is measured on the Mercalli scale. At point 1 on the scale, the earthquake is hardly noticeable. At 6, windows break and cracks appear in walls. At 12, top of the scale, buildings are destroyed.

DID YOU KNOW...
● Great earthquakes have been recorded since the beginning of history? But it is difficult to assess their strength and effects, without the scientific instruments and news communications we have today.
● In 1201 a gigantic quake shook the land around the eastern Mediterranean Sea and across the Middle East? Possibly more than one million people were killed.
● In 1556 another great quake rocked Shensi and neighbouring provinces in China? The death toll could have been more than 800,000.
● There was a large quake in San Francisco in 1906, and the resulting fire almost destroyed the city?
● In 1923 the Kanto Plain of Japan was affected by a huge earthquake that killed about 140,000 people? The nearby coastline showed huge changes, and the sea bed in one place was 400 m deeper after the quake.
● In 1976 the Tangshan earthquake devastated areas of eastern China? The number of people who died has been estimated at anywhere between 250,000 and 750,000.

Can we predict earthquakes?
To an extent, yes. Scientists set up sensitive measuring instruments that detect small earth movements, and strain gauges that show how the stresses build up in the rocks. There are sometimes small "warning shocks" too. But there is no foolproof way of knowing when the "Big One" will come. In western USA, cities such as San Francisco lie along the San Andreas fault line, where an earthquake is expected in the near future.

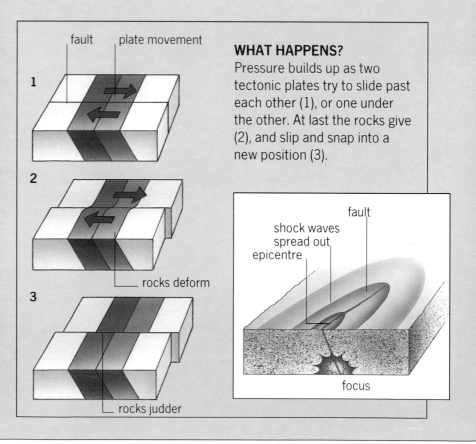

WHAT HAPPENS?
Pressure builds up as two tectonic plates try to slide past each other (1), or one under the other. At last the rocks give (2), and slip and snap into a new position (3).

HOW DEEP DO EARTHQUAKES GO?

They can shake the whole of the crust, up to 50 km deep. The "centre" of the earthquake, where the greatest movement occurs, is usually deep below the surface and is known as the focus. The shock waves spread out from here.

The place on the surface above the focus, where the shock waves seem to be strongest, is the epicentre. The sudden movements may carry the rocks too far. Hours or days later, they spring back and settle, causing aftershocks.

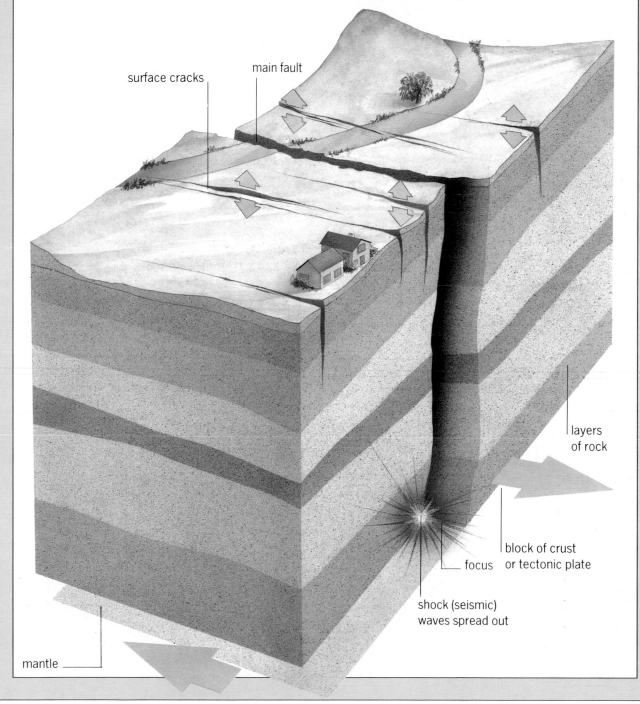

surface cracks

main fault

layers of rock

block of crust or tectonic plate

focus

shock (seismic) waves spread out

mantle

How does rain form?

Rain comes from clouds. A cloud is billions of tiny floating water droplets. As these join and get big and heavy, they fall as rain. This soaks into the ground or runs into rivers and seas. The Sun heats the sea and turns some of it into invisible water vapour. The vapour rises into the cool air and turns back into water droplets. This endless journey is called the water cycle.

SALTY OR FRESH?
● Only one-thirtieth of Earth's water is fresh water. The rest is salty water in seas and oceans.
● Of the fresh water, only one-fifth is liquid. The rest is ice in glaciers and ice sheets. Most of this liquid fresh water is soaked into the ground.

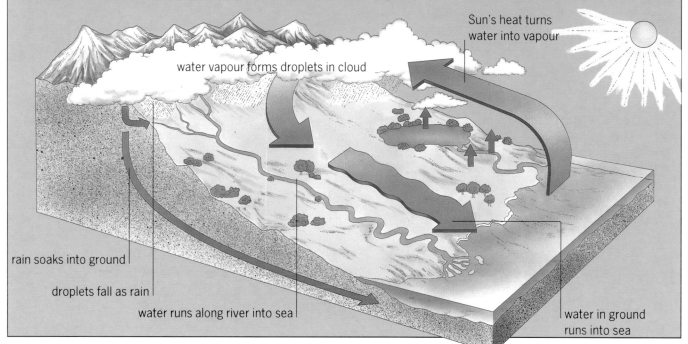

Sun's heat turns water into vapour

water vapour forms droplets in cloud

rain soaks into ground

droplets fall as rain

water runs along river into sea

water in ground runs into sea

What do sea-breakers do?

Winds often blow waves at an angle to the shore. The waves carry pebbles and sand along the beach. Tides pull loose beach material out to sea. Groynes are fences built to prevent the beach being washed away.

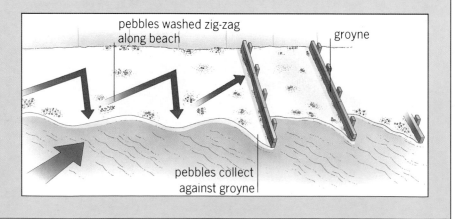

pebbles washed zig-zag along beach

groyne

pebbles collect against groyne

22

Can ice flow like water?

cold mountains

fresh clean snow

moraines –
streaks of soil
and rock scraped
away by ice

snow squashed
into ice

glacier
scoops up
rocks and
soil

crevasses –
cracks in ice

ICE AGES
Four times in the past 2 million years, Earth was much colder. In these Ice Ages, glaciers and ice spread over much of the land.

A long thin piece of ice can bend, just as a long steel rod can bend. Some pieces of ice are hundreds of kilometres long – and they are very bendy! They are called glaciers and are like rivers of ice. When rain falls it forms a river. The water is pulled towards low land by Earth's gravity. In very cold places, such as mountains and polar regions, snow falls and gets squeezed into ice. This is also pulled along and down by gravity, gathering rocks and soil on the way. A glacier flows so slowly you cannot see it move. As the bottom of the glacier reaches a warmer place, it melts and forms a lake.

old melting ice

meltwater lake

snout – tip of glacier

soil and rock dumped
as glacier melts

meltwater stream
under glacier

HOW MUCH ICE?
● One-tenth of the world's land is under glaciers and ice.
● The thickest Antarctic glaciers are 700 m deep.
● The longest glacier is in Antarctica. It is 400 km long and parts are more than 60 km wide.
● The fastest flowing glacier, in Greenland, shifts 20 m a day.

How is sand like the sea?

Because it gets blown along and forms waves! Loose sand rolls and tumbles in the wind, and piles up into wave-shaped hills known as sand dunes. The dunes move along with the wind like waves, but much more slowly. Dunes vary in shape and size largely depending on the size of the sand grains and how strong and steady the wind is.

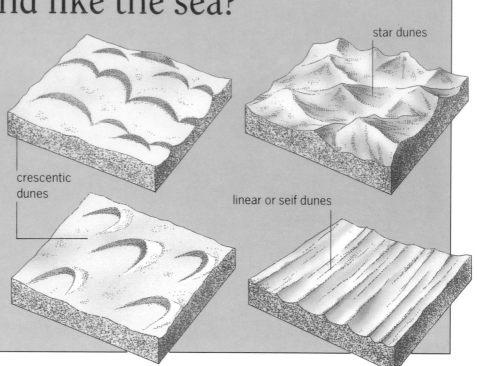

star dunes

crescentic dunes

linear or seif dunes

How do sea caves form?

The waves that are whipped up by the wind alter the landscape of coasts. Sea caves are made where the pounding waves eat away the rocks along the shoreline. Underwater currents and swirling winds may alter the direction of the waves so that they attack either side of a jutting-out headland. Gradually the cliffs crumble. They may leave an isolated block of rock called a stack, or several stacks, called needles.

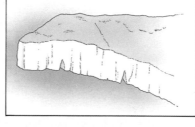

1 The headland juts out into sea, exposed to wind, waves and rain.

2 Waves erode the lower cliffs, making caves and arches.

3 As more rock is worn away, a stack may form at the end.

4 Gradually the headland breaks up and disappears into the sea.

Where do potholers go?

Down under the ground, into an amazing world of underground tunnels, caverns, streams, lakes and waterfalls. These cave systems form mainly in limestone areas, because the slightly acid rainwater trickling into the rocks dissolves away calcium-containing limestone. The water gradually widens tiny holes into tunnels, and cracks into caverns, then finds a new route and leaves them dry. Drips from the roof leave behind minerals that build up into stalactites, "icicles of rock".

DID YOU KNOW...
● In the USA's Mammoth Caves, Kentucky, people are still finding new tunnels and chambers? So far, a total of almost 600 km of tunnels and caves have been mapped. That's longer than the main streets of many cities.
● Cavers have descended more than 1500 m into caves in France and Russia?
● The floor of Krasnohorska cave in the Czech Republic has the tallest stalagmite, at 35 m?

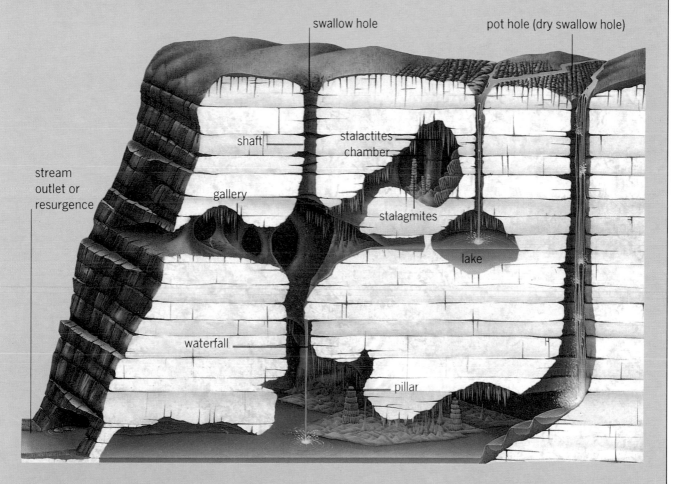

BIGGEST CAVERN?
● The largest single underground chamber is the Sarawak Chamber, Sarawak, South-east Asia. It is 700 m long, 300 m wide, 70 m high.

BIGGEST SYSTEM?
● The world's biggest known cave system is under Mammoth Cave National Park in Kentucky, USA. The caves were found in 1799.

LONGEST UNDERWATER?
● The longest underwater cave network is the Nohoch Na Chich system, in Mexico. Divers explore in pitch blackness and icy cold.

Where does springwater come from?

Out of the ground! In fact, it has soaked and seeped sideways through porous (slightly spongy) rocks, from layers above. Springs and wells form because rainwater soaks into the rocks, and gets trapped in a porous layer between two "waterproof" rock layers. It continues to flow along until it reaches a hole.

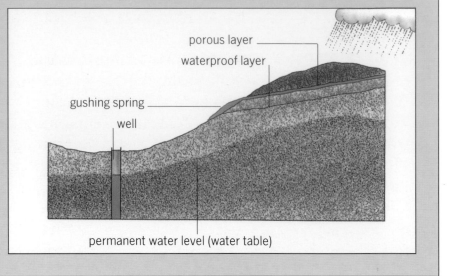

porous layer

waterproof layer

gushing spring

well

permanent water level (water table)

How can I get a free hot bath?

Go to a place such as Iceland, where hot water gushes out of the ground. These fountains of steam and boiling water are called geysers. They come from water heated by the hot rocks, deep down. Be careful! They're very hot!

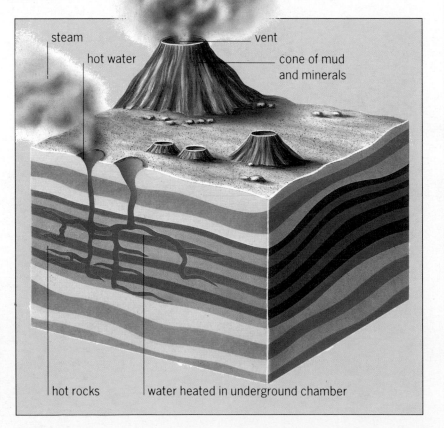

steam

hot water

vent

cone of mud and minerals

hot rocks

water heated in underground chamber

HOW HIGH?

● The highest geyser spout was Waimangu Geyser, in New Zealand, which spurted to 450 m in 1910.
● The tallest active geyser is the Steamboat Geyser in Yellowstone National Park, USA. It spurts water more than 100 m high.

Where can I go back in time, 1,800 million years?

In the Grand Canyon, Arizona, USA. A canyon, chasm or gorge is a deep valley with steep, cliff-like sides. The Grand Canyon has been cut through the ages by the waters of the Colorado River. Today, the river is much smaller and sometimes dries up completely. But through thousands of years it has worn down the stone and eaten its way below the surface, to expose rocks almost two billion years old at the bottom. If you walk with care down the steep path, you travel back in time, seeing fossils of long-dead creatures embedded in the stone.

DID YOU KNOW...

● The entire Grand Canyon is about 350 km long?

● About 170 km of this is in the Grand Canyon National Park, set up in 1919?

● The canyon varies in width from 6 km to 25 km?

● Its greatest depth is 1,620 m?

● Parts of the rim (clifftop edge) on the north side are 300 m higher than those on the south side? This is partly due to rock blocks being lifted up by earth movements.

● The layers of rock cut away by the river include sandstone, limestone and hardened lava? As the Sun moves around during the day, the rocks change colour in spectacular fashion.

● The Grand Canyon is the biggest land chasm? But it is dwarfed by the Labrador basin canyon, in the west Atlantic Ocean, which is 3,500 m long. The deepest land chasm is Peru's El Canyon de Colca. The lowest part is 3,220 m below the rim – a long drop!

Where do rocks come from?

Mostly, from other rocks. The many different minerals that make up various rock types are "recycled" in the Earth as part of a huge and complicated "rock cycle". The three main rock types are igneous, metamorphic and sedimentary.

When any type of rocks gets too hot, it melts. As it cools, it hardens into one of the igneous ("fiery") rocks, such as basalt. The diagrams on the right show different structures made by cooling igneous rocks.

WHERE DOES MARBLE COME FROM?

Rocks that are heated and squeezed, but without melting, change their mineral structure and become metamorphic ("changed form") rocks. One example is marble, used for beautiful statues and buildings. It is made when limestone is altered by the heat and pressure from a nearby lump of hot magma. The limestone nearest to the heat changes its crystal and mineral nature, and becomes marble.

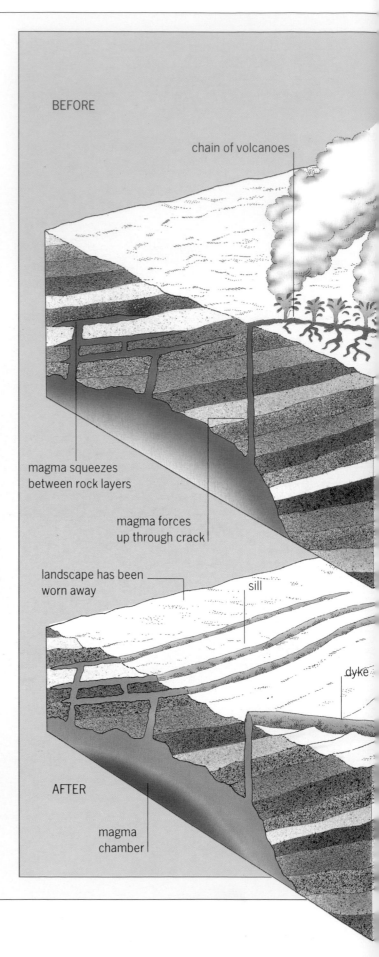

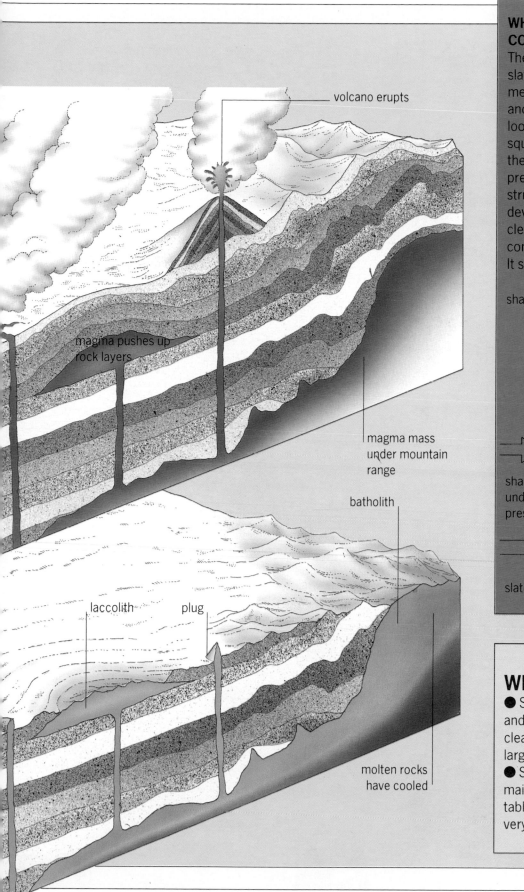

volcano erupts

magma pushes up
rock layers

magma mass
under mountain
range

batholith

laccolith   plug

molten rocks
have cooled

WHERE DO ROOF SLATES COME FROM?

They are cut from thin sheets of slate rock. Slate is an example of a metamorphic rock, made from another rock called shale. The looser, lighter, layered shale was squeezed incredibly hard, deep in the ground. The tremendous pressures altered the mineral structure of the shale, and it developed cracks known as cleavage lines. Gradually it was compressed and made smaller. It slowly turned into slate.

shale layers

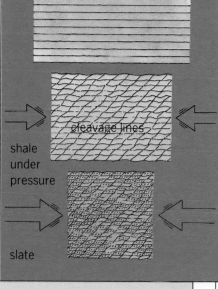

cleavage lines

shale
under
pressure

slate

WHY SLATE?

● Slate is useful for making roof and floor tiles because it splits or cleaves naturally and easily into large, thin sheets.
● Slate is also used to make the main surface for pool and snooker tables because it can be polished very smooth and flat.

What does erosion do?

Day after day the waves, wind, rain, ice, snow, rivers and blowing dust wear away rocks. We see these forces of erosion clearly at work on mountains, but they happen to any rock. They produce flakes and rock particles, which are worn smaller. Most of the bits get swept into rivers, lakes and seas. They sink to the bottom, pile up in thick layers, and gradually get squeezed and stuck together into sedimentary rocks.

WHY "SEDIMENTARY"?
The word sedimentary means "settled down". The settling particles drift down to the bed of a lake or river, or pile up in a desert. They settle in layers, called sediments. Under pressure from more layers that settle above, they get squeezed into solid rocks.

rocks eroded by flowing water

rocks broken down by rain and hail

rocks heat, cool and crack in the Sun

rocks eroded by wind blowing dust and sand

rivers tumble stones and boulders

sand, silt and mud settle in river mouths

How long does it take?

The sedimentation process can take millions of years. The particles are squashed by the weight of more sediments on top of them. Chemical changes also take place. Minerals seep into the water between the bits, and glue them together.

DID YOU KNOW...

● About three-quarters of the rocks exposed at the Earth's surface are sedimentary in origin? But sedimentary rocks form only one-twentieth of the total amount of rock in the Earth's crust.

● Metamorphic rocks form mountain ranges such as the Alps in Europe.

HOW BIG ARE THE BITS?

● Coarse-grained sedimentary rocks contain particles that can be seen with the naked eye, ranging from large boulders to sand grains.

● Medium-grained rocks contain particles that can be seen with a hand lens, as in some sandstones.

● Fine-grained rocks have grains so small that you usually need a microscope to see them. These include shales, clays and mudstones.

● The smallest particles are atoms. They are invisible to the naked eye. These can be arranged in different ways to form different minerals and rocks. Graphite is a soft, slippery, dark rock, used as "lead" in pencils. Diamond is hard, transparent and glittering. Yet they are both made from atoms of carbon.

rocks shattered by frost and ice

rocks rubbed away by glaciers

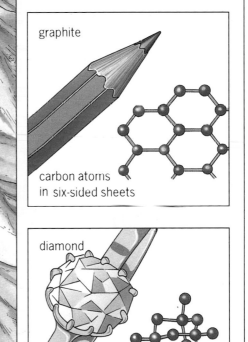

graphite

carbon atoms in six-sided sheets

diamond

carbon atoms in crystal lattice

Where is coal found?

Coal, along with oil and natural gas, are called fossil fuels, and they are types of minerals. They are extracted from the ground by mining or drilling. The world's major coalfields are in North America, Europe and eastern Russia. Oil and natural gas are often found close to coal seams but also exist in large quantities beneath the sea bed (see opposite page).

DID YOU KNOW...
● Small patches of oil, properly known as petroleum, seep to the surface as black sticky lakes? But most oil must be extracted by drilling wells.
● Some oil wells are more than 1,000 m deep.
● Coal comes either from the surface, known as open-cast mining, or from under the ground by digging deep mines?
● The biggest open-cast coal mine is in Germany? It covers 21 sq km and is 350 m deep, and mines the soft brown coal known as lignite.

● "large" coal production
· "small" coal production
● "large" oil production
· "small" oil production

BIGGEST COALFIELDS?
These are in the Appalachian region of the USA, Nova Scotia, the Donetz fields of southern Russia, Silesia, and the Ruhr and other regions in Europe. The USA has about one-third of the world's coal that can be mined.

BIGGEST OILFIELD?
The largest single oilfield is in Saudi Arabia. It is known as the Ghawar Field, and is 240 km long and 40 km wide. Most of the world's oil now comes from the Middle East area. The North Sea also has large reserves.

BIGGEST GAS FIELD?
The largest concentrated gas field is at Urengoi in Russia. It holds an estimated 7 million million cubic metres of natural gas. At the present rate of use, it will all be gone in 40 years. Fossil fuels are not renewable.

Why is oil called "black gold"?

Because if you have a big oilfield under your back yard or garden, you could become very rich! Crude oil, or petroleum, is thick, sticky, smelly – and very valuable. It is made into a vast array of substances that are vital in today's world. Petrol, diesel, jet fuel (kerosene), plastics, paints, fertilizers, oils and lubricants – the list goes on and on. Modern life would grind to a halt without them. So finding an oilfield is like having a gold mine. No wonder that the petroleum companies spend millions every year on searching for oil and gas.

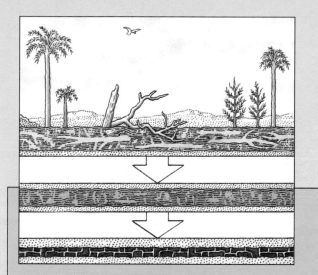

HOW WAS COAL FORMED?
Prehistoric plants died and were quickly buried, rather than rotting away. More plants died on top, squashing those below into the rock we call coal.

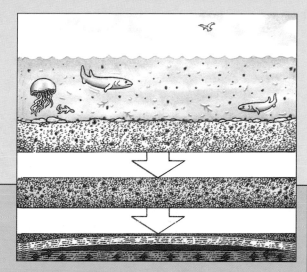

HOW WAS OIL FORMED?
Sea organisms died and sank to the bottom. More sediments collected on top. The dead bodies were squashed and collected as oil droplets in the rock.

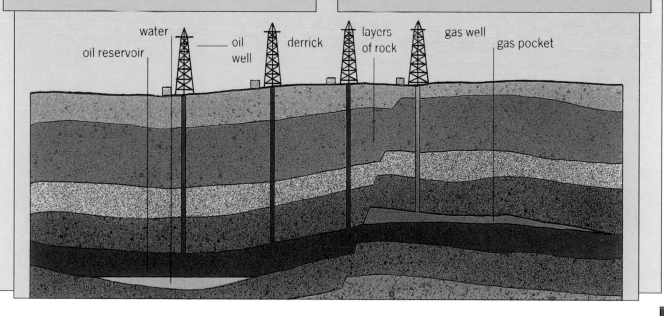

water
oil reservoir
oil well
derrick
layers of rock
gas well
gas pocket

What happens when coal runs out?

Coal, oil and gas are unsustainable resources. This means we are using them millions of times faster that they can re-form themselves. So their amounts in the Earth are not being renewed or sustained. They will run out, unless we cut back incredibly on their use. But there are renewable sources of energy!

WILL WIND DO?

Wind, driven by heat from the Sun, is a renewable form of energy. Windmills use its power to raise water for irrigation, grind corn, and turn machines. High-tech versions can produce electricity, but they cover windy areas with unsightly blades and sails. Computer-controlled sails could save engine fuel for seacraft.

windmill turned to face wind

sails made from lightweight carbon-fibre and composite materials

What will never run out?

Immense amounts of energy reach the Earth every day – from the Sun. The Sun's energy warms air and creates winds that may drive a new generation of windmills and sailing ships. Sunlight can be captured and focused by huge banks of mirrors, to make heat for an electricity power station. Hydroelectric power stations use the energy of running water. Even this comes from the Sun, which evaporated the water into vapour and sent it into the atmosphere, to fall as rain.

water flowing through dam turns turbine blades to generate electricity

WILL SOLAR ENERGY DO?

Solar power stations generate electricity directly from the Sun's light and heat. The biggest is in the Mojave Desert, California, USA. It should produce over 600 megawatts of electricity – enough for a town of one million people.

The problem is, if the Sun goes in, the power generation ceases.

mirrors are angled to focus rays at one point

When did life on Earth begin?

At least 3.5 billion years ago (that's 3,500,000,000 years), from the evidence of the remains of living things in the rocks, known as fossils. The earliest fossils are microscopic rounded remains. They look as if they were made by living things similar to today's bacteria, a type of microbe, or today's blue-green algae, a type of plant-like organism. The time chart shows how living things have evolved since then.

WHO STUDIES FOSSILS?

Anyone can look for fossils, and learn about them. The expert scientific study of fossils is called paleontology. This overlaps with the study of rocks, and how they form and change, which is termed petrology. The general study of the Earth's crust and landscapes is known as geology.

ERA	PERIOD	Millions of Years Ago
CENOZOIC ("recent life")	Quaternary	2
CENOZOIC ("recent life")	Tertiary	65
MESOZOIC ("middle life")	Cretaceous	144
MESOZOIC ("middle life")	Jurassic	213
MESOZOIC ("middle life")	Triassic	248
PALEOZOIC ("ancient life")	Permian	286
PALEOZOIC ("ancient life")	Carboniferous	360
PALEOZOIC ("ancient life")	Devonian	408
PALEOZOIC ("ancient life")	Silurian	438
PALEOZOIC ("ancient life")	Ordovician	505
PALEOZOIC ("ancient life")	Cambrian	590
PALEOZOIC ("ancient life")	Precambrian	

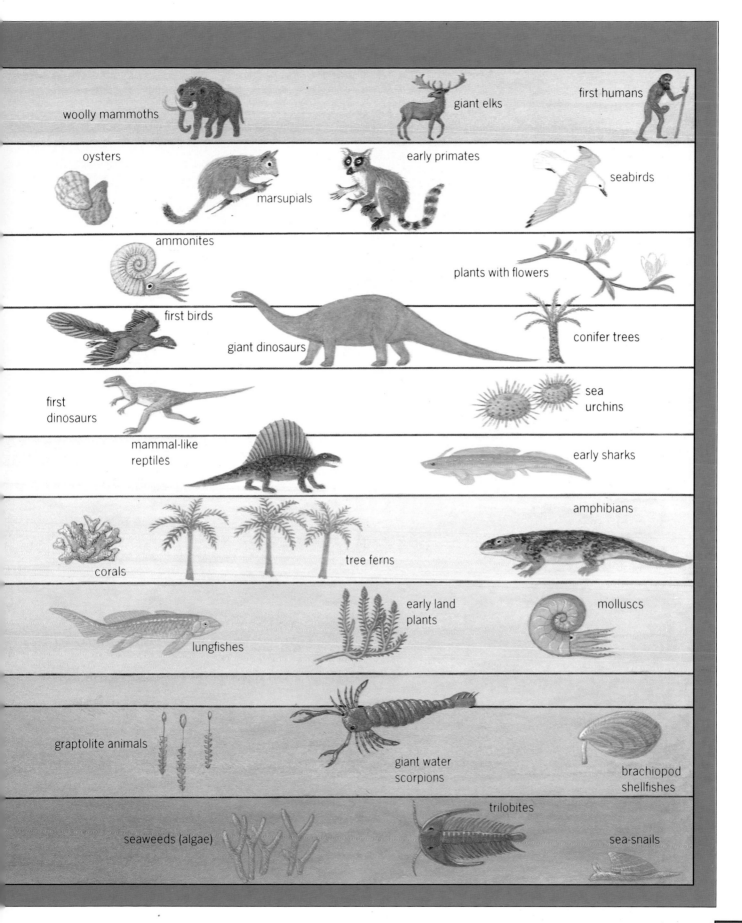

woolly mammoths

giant elks

first humans

oysters

marsupials

early primates

seabirds

ammonites

plants with flowers

first birds

giant dinosaurs

conifer trees

first dinosaurs

sea urchins

mammal-like reptiles

early sharks

amphibians

corals

tree ferns

lungfishes

early land plants

molluscs

graptolite animals

giant water scorpions

brachiopod shellfishes

trilobites

seaweeds (algae)

sea-snails

Exactly what is a fossil?

Fossils are the remains of living things that died long ago, which have been buried in the rocks and turned into stone. Usually only the hard parts become fossils, such as bones, teeth, claws, shells, tree bark, seeds, and leaf veins. The soft parts rot away quickly. The hard parts get buried in sediments of sand or mud, usually on the bed of a lake or sea. As the sediments turn into rock, the parts turn into rock, as well. So fossils are found only in sedimentary rock, not in igneous or metamorphic rock.

WHAT IS A CAST FOSSIL?
A shellfish lived on the sea bed, millions of years ago (1). It died, the flesh inside rotted, and the shell was covered by sandy sediment (2). The sediment turned to rock, but the shell slowly decayed and disappeared. It left a hole shaped like itself, called a mould (3). Water seeped through the rock, bringing minerals that gradually filled the hole (4). Finally the mineral lump became a solid-rock copy of the original shell (5). This copy is known as a cast fossil.

CAN SOFT WORMS FOSSILIZE?
Yes. In exceptional circumstances, soft-bodied animals can be buried quickly, before they rot away. This happened about 550 million years ago to form fossils in Canada as shown below.

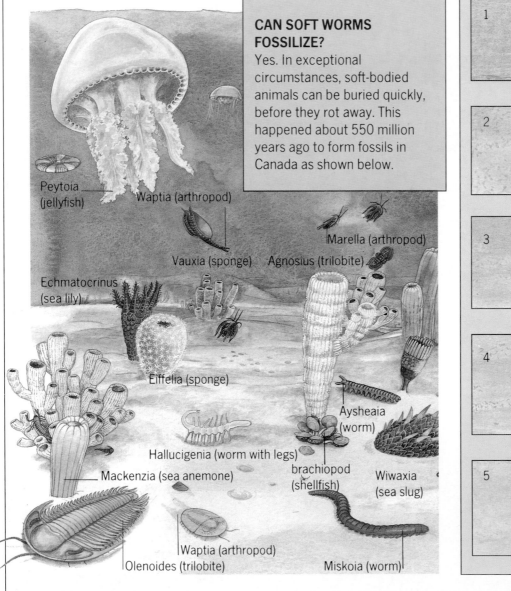

Peytoia (jellyfish)
Waptia (arthropod)
Marella (arthropod)
Vauxia (sponge)
Agnosius (trilobite)
Echmatocrinus (sea lily)
Eiffelia (sponge)
Aysheaia (worm)
Hallucigenia (worm with legs)
brachiopod (shellfish)
Wiwaxia (sea slug)
Mackenzia (sea anemone)
Waptia (arthropod)
Olenoides (trilobite)
Miskoia (worm)

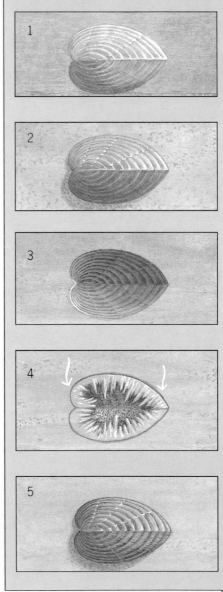

1

2

3

4

5

How old are fossils?

A fossil is as old as the rock it is embedded in. You can tell the age of the rock by various means, such as its type, the amounts of very weak radioactivity it gives off, and the characteristic types of rocks above and below it, as shown in the diagram. For example, thick coal rocks were formed mainly in the Carboniferous period, about 300 million years ago. Some animals and plants were only alive at certain times, so fossils can be dated like this.

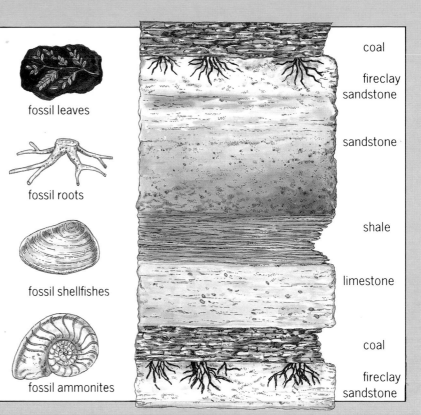

fossil leaves

fossil roots

fossil shellfishes

fossil ammonites

coal
fireclay
sandstone
sandstone
shale
limestone
coal
fireclay
sandstone

Where can you find fossils?

Anywhere that suitable sedimentary rocks are exposed. Good places are beaches, cliffs, quarries, and road and railroad cuttings. At some places, such as Lyme Regis in Dorset, England, the beach is almost full of fossils. A young lady called Mary Anning became the first full-time fossil-hunter there, around 1810.

Where does it rain daily?

In a rainforest! Some rainforests have a dry season of a few weeks. But in most rainforests it rains every day or every few days. The tropical rainforests are found along the Equator. Trade winds bring moist air all year round. The weather is warm and damp, creating ideal conditions for life to flourish. Tropical rainforests are the richest places for life on Earth. Thousands of kinds of butterflies and other insects, worms, frogs, snakes and lizards, birds and mammals live among the branches and leaves, and in the dead leaves and soil on the forest floor. The picture shows a selection of creatures from different rainforests.

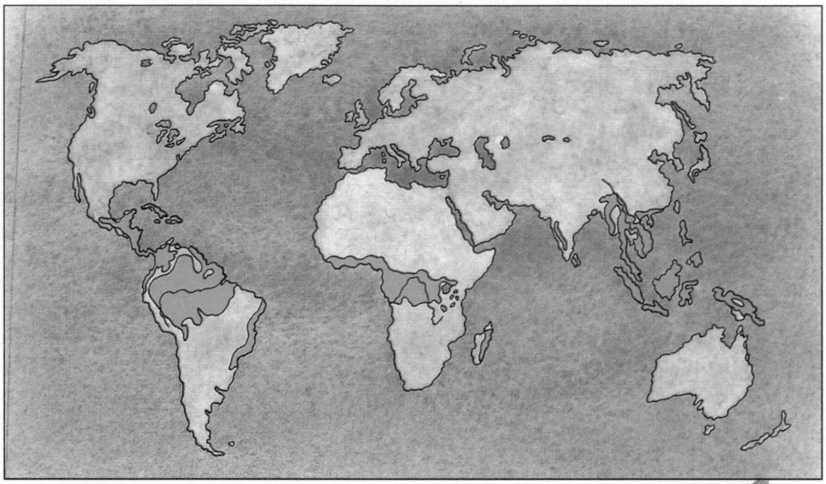

HOW WET OR HOT?
● Most tropical rainforests have 2,500 mm or more of rain each year. The wettest have more than 10,000 mm (10 m). This compares with about 600 mm for London, England.
● Since they are in the tropics, there is little seasonal change in the temperatures. Most tropical rainforests are about 20-28°C through the year. (There are other rainforests outside the tropics, as in New Zealand.)

KEY
1 scarlet macaw
2 toucan
3 arrow-poison frog
4 Jackson's chameleon
5 caiman
6 orang-utan
7 hummingbird

Why are some places grassy?

Grasslands grow where the climate is very warm but too dry for forests of trees. Grass can withstand periods of drought, when there is no rain. It also grows back well after fires, which often sweep across the grassland after lightning strikes. The picture shows a selection of creatures from the African grasslands.

Grasslands tend to occur between the forests of the tropics, and the deserts or woodlands farther north and south.

WHAT'S IN A NAME?
Grasslands have different names in different parts of the world:
● In Africa they are called savannahs or savannas. These grasslands have some trees.
● In Asia they are known as steppes.
● In North America they are named prairies or plains.
● In South America they are termed pampas.

WHAT LIVES IN THE WOODLANDS?

Many familiar animals in Europe, North America and northern Asia live in deciduous and evergreen woodlands. This illustration shows the natural wildlife of a European deciduous woodland. But millions of trees have been cut down for timber, used in building and for fuel, and to clear the land for crops and grazing animals. Many of the original types of animals and plants have disappeared.

Where's the coldest place on Earth?

The lowest temperatures have been recorded on the great southern continent of Antarctica. At Vostok Base, it has been as low as minus 89°C. (Water freezes at 0°C.) It is almost as cold near the North Pole, where temperatures of minus 68°C have been detected in Siberia.

THE NORTH POLE
There is no land at the North Pole. The northern ice cap floats in the Arctic Ocean.

WHAT LIVES IN THE ARCTIC?
At the North and South Poles themselves, no living things can survive. But in the oceans and lands around the poles, known as the polar regions, life is plentiful. Some of the animals are shown here. The mammals and birds have thick fur or feathers, and thick layers of fatty blubber under the skin, to keep in body warmth. In the long, dark winter, some of them migrate to warmer places nearer the Equator.

WHY IS IT COLD ON MOUNTAIN TOPS?
Going up a mountain is like travelling from the Equator towards the North or South Pole. This is because as you go higher into the atmosphere, the temperature goes lower. On a mountain in the tropics, there are forests on the foothills. As you climb the slopes, broadleaved trees give way to conifers, then sparse alpine grasses and scrub, and finally the ice and cold of the summit.

temperate forest

snow and ice

conifer forest

tree line

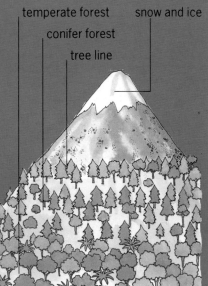

Do polar bears eat penguins?

In a zoo, perhaps they might. But not in nature. Polar bears live in the far north of the Arctic. Penguins live in the far south of the Antarctic. So the two would never meet. Great whales such as the blue whale and humpback visit both polar regions during their short summers, to feed on the plentiful sea life. The Arctic tern nests in the Arctic summer. Then it flies around the world and spends the next few months in the summer of the Antarctic.

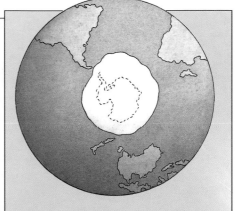

THE SOUTH POLE
The southern ice cap covers the continent of Antarctica and spreads into the oceans around.

WHO LIVES IN THE ANTARCTIC?
Antarctica is mostly covered with ice hundreds of metres thick. Only a few little flowers and mosses, and a few small animals such as tiny insects, can survive. But the seas around are teeming with life, especially during the brief summer. There are fish and squid, which are eaten by seals and penguins.

INDEX